SCIENTOLOGY

Making the World a Better Place

Founded and developed by L. Ron Hubbard, Scientology is an applied religious philosophy which offers an exact route through which anyone can regain the truth and simplicity of his spiritual self.

Scientology consists of specific axioms that define the underlying causes and principles of existence and a vast area of observations in the humanities, a philosophic body that literally applies to the entirety of life.

This broad body of knowledge resulted in two applications of the subject: first, a technology for man to increase his spiritual awareness and attain the freedom sought by many great philosophic teachings; and, second, a great number of fundamental principles men can use to improve their lives. In fact, in this second application, Scientology offers nothing less than practical methods to better *every* aspect of our existence—means to create new ways of life. And from this comes the subject matter you are about to read.

Compiled from the writings of L. Ron Hubbard, the data presented here is but one of the tools which can be found in *The Scientology Handbook*. A comprehensive guide, the handbook contains numerous applications of Scientology which can be used to improve many other areas of life.

In this booklet, the editors have augmented the data with a short introduction, practical exercises and examples of successful application.

Courses to increase your understanding and further materials to broaden your knowledge are available at your nearest Scientology church or mission, listed at the back of this booklet.

Many new phenomena about man and life are described in Scientology, and so you may encounter terms in these pages you are not familiar with. These are described the first time they appear and in the glossary at the back of the booklet.

Scientology is for use. It is a practical philosophy, something one *does*. Using this data, you *can* change conditions.

Millions of people who want to do something about the conditions they see around them have applied this knowledge. They know that life can be improved. And they know that Scientology works.

Use what you read in these pages to help yourself and others and you will too.

CHURCH OF SCIENTOLOGY INTERNATIONAL

*Consider this for a moment: In all your schooling, did anyone ever teach you **how** to study something?*

*Today, people are graduating school unable to read or write at a level adequate to hold a job or deal with life. It is a huge problem. It is not that subjects cannot be learned; what isn't taught is **how** to learn. It is the missing step in all education.*

L. Ron Hubbard filled this gaping hole by supplying the first and only technology of how to study. He discovered the laws on which learning is based and developed workable methods for anyone to apply. He called this subject "Study Technology."

This technology provides an understanding of the basics of learning and supplies exact ways to overcome all the pitfalls one can encounter during study.

*Study Technology is not speed-reading or memory tricks. These have not been proven to raise one's ability to comprehend what was studied or to raise literacy. Study Technology shows **how** one studies in order to comprehend a subject so one can **apply** it.*

*Contained herein is only a small portion of the entire body of Study Technology developed by Mr. Hubbard. Regardless, this brief overview contains fundamentals which you can use to study more effectively. With this technology, **any** subject can be learned by **anyone.**■*

WHY STUDY?

With all the emphasis placed on education in our society it is remarkable to realize that there has never been an actual technology of study or a technology of education. That sounds very far-fetched but it is true. There was a *school* technology, but it didn't have too much to do with *education*. It consisted of the technology of how you go to school, how you get taught and how you get examined, but there was no actual technology of education or *study*. Lacking such a technology, people find it difficult to achieve their goals. Knowing how to study is vitally important to *anyone*.

The first little gate that has to be opened to embark upon study is the willingness to know. If that gate remains closed, then one is liable to get into such things as a total memorized, word-for-word system of education, which will not result in the gain of any knowledge. Such a system only produces graduates who can possibly parrot back facts, but without any real understanding or ability to do anything with what they have been taught.

For what purpose, then, does one study? Until you clarify that, you cannot make an intelligent activity of it.

Some students study for the examination. The student is thinking to himself, "How will I repeat this back when I am asked a certain question?" or "How will I pass the examination?" That is complete folly, but unfortunately is what many students have done in a university.

Take the man who has been building houses for a long time, who one day gets an assistant who has just been trained in the university to build houses. He goes mad! The *academically* trained man has been studying it for years, yet knows nothing about it. And the *practical* man doesn't know why this is.

The reason why is that the man who just went through the university studied all of his materials so that he could be examined on them; he didn't study them to build houses. The man who has been out there on a practical line is not necessarily superior in the long run, but he certainly is able to get houses built, because all of *his* study is on the basis of "How do I apply this to house building?" Every time he picks up an ad or literature or anything else, he is asking the question throughout the entirety of his reading, "How can I apply this to what I'm doing?"

That is the basic and important difference between *practical* study and *academic* study.

This is why some people fail in practice after they graduate.

Instead of looking at data and thinking, "Is this going to be on the exam?" one would do much better to ask oneself, "How can I apply this material?" or "How can I really use this?"

By doing this a person will get much more out of what he studies and will be able to put what he studies to actual use.

The Student Who Knows All About It

On the subject of learning itself, the first datum to learn and the primary obstacle to overcome is: *You cannot study a subject if you think you know all about it to begin with.*

A student who thinks he knows all there is to know about a subject will not be able to learn anything in it.

A person might already be familiar with a subject from previous experience and, having had success in that field, now has the idea that he knows all about it. If such a person then took a course in that subject, he would be studying *through* a screen of "I know all about this."

With that obstacle in the way, one can become completely bogged down in his studies and not make forward progress.

This is true for a student of any subject.

If one can decide that he does not already know everything about a subject and can say to himself, "Here is something to study, let's study it," he can overcome this obstacle and be able to learn.

This is a very, very important datum for any student. If he understands this and applies it, the gateway to knowledge is wide open to him.

BARRIERS TO STUDY

Being a successful student requires more than just a willingness to learn, however. Pitfalls do exist and students must know *how* to effectively learn in order to overcome them.

It has been discovered that there are three definite barriers which can block a person's ability to study and thus his ability to be educated. These barriers actually produce different sets of physical and mental reactions.

If one knows and understands what these barriers are and how to handle them, his ability to study and learn will be greatly increased.

The First Barrier: Absence of Mass

In Study Technology, we refer to the *mass* and the *significance* of a subject. By *mass* we mean the actual physical objects, the things of life. The *significance* of a subject is the meaning or ideas or theory of it.

Education attempted in the absence of the *mass* in which the technology will be involved is hard on a student.

If you were studying about tractors, the mass would be a tractor. You could study a textbook all about tractors, how to operate the controls, the different types of attachments that can be used—in other words, all the significance—but can you imagine how little you would understand if you had never actually seen a tractor?

Such an absence of mass can actually make a student feel squashed. It can make him feel bent, sort of dizzy, sort of dead, bored and exasperated.

Photographs or motion pictures can be helpful because they represent a promise or hope of the mass. But if one is studying about tractors, the printed page and the spoken word are not a substitute for an actual tractor!

Not having the mass of what one is studying about can make a student feel bent, dizzy, dead, bored and exasperated. The printed page is not a substitute for the actual mass.

MASS

SIGNIFICANCE

Educating a person in a mass that he does not have and which is not available can produce some uncomfortable and distracting physical reactions.

If you were trying to teach someone all about tractors but you did not show him any tractors or let him experience the mass of a tractor, he would wind up with a face that felt squashed, with headaches and with his stomach feeling funny. He would feel dizzy from time to time and often his eyes would hurt.

Students of any age can run into this barrier. Let us say that little Johnny is having an awful time at school with his arithmetic. You find out that he had an arithmetic problem that involved apples, but he never had any apples on his desk to count. Get him some apples and give each one of them a number. Now he has a number of apples in front of him—there is no longer a theoretical number of apples.

The point is that you could trace Johnny's problem back to an absence of mass and remedy it by supplying the mass; or you could supply an object or a reasonable substitute.

This barrier to study—the studying of something without its mass ever being around—produces these distinctly recognizable reactions.

Remedying an Absence of Mass

As not everyone studying has the actual mass available, useful tools to remedy a lack of mass have been developed. These come under the subject of demonstration.

Demonstration comes from the Latin *demonstrare*: "to point out, show, prove."

The *Chambers 20th Century Dictionary* includes the following definition of *demonstrate*: "to teach, expound or exhibit by practical means."

In order to supply mass, one would *do* a demonstration. One way of accomplishing this is with a "demonstration kit." A "demo kit," as it is called, is composed of various small objects such as corks, caps, paper clips, pen tops, rubber bands, etc. A student can use a demo kit to represent the things he is studying and help him to understand concepts.

Demonstrating a concept with various small objects adds mass to what a person is studying. This increases understanding.

If a student ran into something he couldn't quite figure out, demonstrating the idea with a demo kit would assist him to understand it.

Anything can be demonstrated with a demo kit: ideas, objects, interrelationships or how something works. One simply uses these small objects to represent the various parts of something he is studying about. The objects can be moved about in relation to each other to show the mechanics and actions of a given concept.

Another means of demonstrating something is by sketching.

Someone sitting at his office desk trying to work something out can take a pencil and paper and, by sketching out or drawing graphs of what he was working with, get a grip on it.

There is a rule which goes *if you cannot demonstrate something in two dimensions, you have it wrong.* It is an arbitrary rule—based on judgment or discretion—but is very workable.

Sketching helps one to work things out.

This rule is used in engineering and architecture. If it cannot be worked out simply and clearly in two dimensions, there is something wrong and it couldn't be built.

Sketching and two-dimensional representation is all part of demonstration and of working something out.

A third means of supplying mass to clarify principles is through the use of modeling clay to make a *clay demonstration,* or "clay demo," of a principle or concept.

The purpose of clay demonstration is:

1. to make the materials being studied real to the student,

2. to give a proper balance of mass and significance,

3. to teach the student to *apply*.

The whole theory of clay demonstrations is that they add mass.

Objects, actions, thoughts, ideas, relationships or anything else can be demonstrated in clay.

A student needs mass in order to understand something. Without it, he only has thoughts or mental concepts. Given mass, he can sort it out because he has mass and space in which to then envision the concept he is studying.

Demo kit demonstrations work on this principle too, only a clay demonstration more closely represents the thing being demonstrated and provides more mass.

Any student can use clay to demonstrate an action, definition, object or principle. He sits at a table set up with different colors of modeling clay for his use. He demonstrates the object or principle in clay, labeling each part. The clay *shows* the thing. It is *not* just a blob of clay with a label on it. Small strips of paper are used for labels.

For example, say a student wants to demonstrate a pencil. He makes a thin roll of clay which is surrounded by another layer of clay—the thin roll sticking slightly out of one end. On the other end goes a small cylinder of clay. The roll is labeled "lead." The outer layer is labeled "wood." The small cylinder is labeled "rubber."

Simplicity is the keynote.

Anything can be demonstrated in clay if one works at it. And just by working on *how* to demonstrate it or make it into clay and labels brings about renewed understanding.

In the phrase "How do I represent it in clay?" is contained the secret of the teaching. If one can represent it in clay, one understands it. If one can't, one really doesn't understand what it is. So clay and labels work only if the term or things are truly understood. And working them out in clay brings about an understanding of them.

Art is no object in doing clay demo work. The forms are crude.

Each separate thing made in a clay demo is labeled, no matter how crude the label is. Students usually do labels on scraps of paper or light cardboard written on with a ballpoint. When making a label, a point is put on one end, making it easy to stick the label into the clay.

The procedure should go: student makes one object, labels it, makes another object, labels it, makes a third object and puts a label on it and so on in sequence. This comes from the datum that optimum learning requires an equal balance of mass and significance and that too much of one without the other can make the student feel bad. If a student makes all the masses of his demonstration at once, without labeling them, he is sitting there with all those significances stacking up in his mind instead of putting down each one (in the form of a label) as he goes. The correct procedure is to label each mass as one goes along.

Any object or principle or action can be represented by a piece of clay and a label. The mass parts are done by clay, the significance or thought parts by label.

Directions of motion or travel are usually indicated with little arrows. The arrow can be made out of clay or it can be made as another type of label. This can become important. Lack of clarity in the demo about which way what is going or which way what is flowing can make the demo unrecognizable.

A person's understanding can be assisted greatly when he works something out and puts it down in physical form.

Clay demos must be large. One of the purposes of clay demonstrations is to make the materials being studied *real* to the student. If a student's clay demo is small (less mass), it may not be sufficiently real to the person. *Big* clay demos are more successful in terms of increasing student understanding.

A well-done clay demo, which actually does demonstrate, will produce a marvelous change in the student. And he will retain the data.

Each of these three methods of remedying an absence of mass—using a demo kit, sketching and clay demonstrations—should be used liberally in any educational activity. They can make a big difference in how well a student learns and can apply what he has studied.

The Second Barrier: Too Steep a Gradient

A *gradient* is a gradual approach to something taken step by step, level by level, each step or level being, of itself, easily attainable—so that finally, complicated and difficult activities can be achieved with relative ease. The term *gradient* also applies to each of the steps taken in such an approach.

When one hits too steep a gradient in studying a subject, a sort of confusion or reelingness (a state of mental swaying or unsteadiness) results. This is the second barrier to study.

The remedy for too steep a gradient is to cut back the gradient. Find out when the person was not confused about what he was studying and then find out what *new* action he undertook. Find out what he felt he understood well just *before* he got all confused.

Learning to ride a bicycle is often too steep a gradient for a child.

But a set of training wheels makes it possible for him to progress. This is a proper gradient.

You will discover that there is something in this area—the part he'd felt he understood well—which he did not really understand.

When this is cleared up, the student will be able to progress again.

When a person is found to be terribly confused on the second action he was supposed to know or do, it is safe to assume that he never really understood the *first* action.

This barrier is most recognizable and most applicable when engaged in *doingness*—performing some action or activity—as opposed to just academic or intellectual study.

The Third–and Most Important–Barrier: The Misunderstood Word

The third and most important barrier to study is the misunderstood word. A misunderstood word is a word which is *not* understood or *wrongly* understood.

An entirely different set of physical reactions can occur when one reads past words he does not understand. Going on past a word that was not understood gives one a distinctly blank feeling or a washed-out feeling.

A "not-there" feeling and a sort of nervous hysteria (excessive anxiety) can follow that.

The confusion or inability to grasp or learn comes *after* a word that the person did not have defined and understood.

The misunderstood word is much more important than the other two barriers. The misunderstood word establishes aptitude and lack of aptitude; this is what psychologists have been trying to test for years without recognizing what it was.

This is all that many study difficulties go back to. Studying past misunderstood words produces such a vast range of mental effects that it itself is the prime factor involved with stupidity and many other unwanted conditions.

If a person didn't have misunderstood words, his *talent* might or might not be present, but his *doingness* in that subject would be present.

There are two specific phenomena which stem from misunderstood words.

First Phenomenon

When a student misses understanding a word, the section right after that word is a blank in his memory.

You can always trace back to the word just before the blank, get it understood and find miraculously that the former blank area is not now blank in the material you are studying.

It is pure magic.

When a person is reading down a page...

...and goes past a word for which he has no definition...

...the section after the misunderstood word will be blank in his memory. The misunderstood word is the most important barrier to successful study.

Have you ever had the experience of coming to the end of a page and realizing you didn't know what you had read? Somewhere earlier on that page you went past a word that you had no definition for or an incorrect definition for.

Here is an example: "It was found that when the crepuscule arrived the children were quieter and when it was not present, they were much livelier." What happens is you think you do not understand the whole idea, but the inability to understand comes entirely from the one word you could not define, *crepuscule,* which means twilight or darkness.

Second Phenomenon

A misunderstood definition or a not-comprehended definition or an undefined word can even cause a person to give up studying a subject and leave a course or class. Leaving in this way is called a *blow*.

We have all known people who enthusiastically started on a course of study only to find out some time later that the person dropped the study because it was "boring" or "it wasn't what they thought it would be." They were going to learn a skill or go to night school and get their degree but never followed through. No matter how reasonable their excuses, the fact is they dropped the subject or left the course. This is a blow. A person blows for only one primary reason—the misunderstood word.

A person does not necessarily blow because of the other barriers to study—lack of mass or too steep a gradient. These simply produce physical phenomena. But the misunderstood word can cause a student to blow.

There is a definite sequence of actions following a misunderstood word:

When a word is not grasped, the student then goes into a noncomprehension (blankness) of things immediately after. This is followed by the student's solution for the blank condition which is to *individuate* from it—meaning to separate himself from it and withdraw from involvement with it.

Now that the student is separated from the area he was studying, he does not really care what he does with regard to the subject or related things or activities. This is the attitude—being separate or different from—which precedes doing something harmful to something or someone.

For example, a student in school who has gone past misunderstood words in a course will not care about what happens in class, will probably bad-mouth the subject to his friends and may even damage class equipment or lose his textbook.

However, people are basically good. When an individual commits a harmful act, he then makes an effort to restrain himself from committing more harmful acts. This is followed by his finding ways he has been "wronged" by others, in order to justify his actions, and by complaints, faultfinding and a "look-what-you-did-to-me" attitude. These factors justify, in the student's mind, a departure or blow.

But most educational systems, frowning on blows as they do, cause the student to really withdraw himself from the study subject (whatever he was studying) and set up in its place mental machinery which can receive and give back sentences and phrases. A person can set up mental machinery when he becomes disinterested in what he is doing but feels he has to continue doing it.

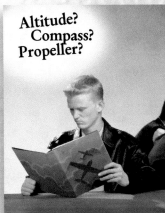

Altitude?
Compass?
Propeller?

A person often starts study of a new subject with great eagerness.

However, if he accumulates misunderstood words, his interest wanes.

If he does not find these and get them defined, he will lose interest entirely and abandon the subject. This is called a blow.

We now have "the quick student who somehow never applies what he learns," also called a *glib student.*

The specific phenomenon then is that a student can study some words and give them back and yet be no participant to the action. The student gets A+ on exams but can't apply the data.

The thoroughly dull (stupid) student is just stuck in the noncomprehend blankness following some misunderstood word. He won't be able to demonstrate his materials with a demo kit or in clay, and such difficulties are a sure sign that a misunderstood word exists.

The "very bright" student who yet can't use the data is *not there* at all. He has long since ceased to confront (face without flinching or avoiding) the subject matter or the subject.

The cure for either of these conditions of "bright noncomprehension" or "dull" is to find the missing word.

This discovery of the importance of the misunderstood word actually opens the door to education. And although this barrier to study has been given last, it is the most important one.

CLEARING WORDS

A misunderstood word will remain misunderstood until one *clears* the meaning of the word. Once the word is fully understood by the person, it is said to be *cleared*.

The procedures used to locate and clear up words the student has misunderstood in his studies are called *Word Clearing*. The first thing to learn is the exact procedure to clear any word or symbol one comes across in reading or studying that he does not understand. All Word Clearing technology uses this procedure.

Steps to Clear a Word

1. Have a dictionary to hand while reading so that you can clear any misunderstood word or symbol you come across. A simple but good dictionary can be found that does not itself contain large words within the definitions of the words which themselves have to be cleared.

2. When you come across a word or symbol that you do not understand, look it up in a dictionary and look rapidly over the definitions to find the one which applies to the context in which the word was misunderstood. Read that definition and make up sentences using the word with that meaning until you have a clear concept of that meaning of the word. This could require ten or more sentences.

3. Then clear each of the other definitions of that word, using each one in sentences until you clearly understand each definition.

When a word has several different definitions, you cannot limit your understanding of the word to one definition only and call the word "understood." You must be able to understand the word when, at a later date, it is used in a different way.

Don't, however, clear the technical or specialized definitions (math, biology, etc.) or obsolete (no longer used) or archaic (ancient and no longer in general use) definitions unless the word is being used that way in the context where it was misunderstood. Doing so may lead off into many other words contained in those definitions and greatly slow one's study progress.

If a person encounters difficulty with what he is reading…

…there will be a misunderstood word earlier in his text. He must go back and locate the word.

Felis domesticus?

When he looks up the word in a dictionary and defines it…

Felis domesticus

…the difficulty vanishes and he can progress.

Example of Clearing a Word

I know that he has ne~~~
jobs. He used to clean chimneys for
a living. It is actually quite
extraordinary for a man his age.
~~~rs are in their

■ *Let's say that you are reading the sentence,
"He used to clean chimneys for a living," and
you're not sure what "chimneys" means.*

unreal, imaginary
chimney 1. A flue for the smoke or
gases from a fire. 2. A glass tube
~~~ound the flame of a lamp. 3. A vent
~~~ [OFr. LL

■ *You find it in the dictionary and look
through the definitions for the one that
applies. It says "a flue for the smoke or gases
from a fire."*

fluctuation **n**
flue (floo) **n** 1. a channel or passage
for smoke, air or gases. 2. Any duct
~~~ passage for air, gas or the like. 3. A
~~~ [OFr.

■ *You're not sure what "flue" means so you
look that up. It says "a channel or passage for
smoke, air or gases." That fits and makes
sense, so you use it in some sentences until
you have a clear concept of it.*

~~~
for smoke, air or gases.
2. Any duct or passage for air,
gas or the like. 3. A tube, especially a
large one. [OFr. *fluie,* a flowing]

■ *"Flue" in this dictionary has other
definitions, each of which you would clear
and use in sentences.*

smoke, ~~~
passage for air, gas or the like. ~~~
tube, especially a large one. [OFr. *fluie,*
a flowing]
~~~ an organ pipe

■ *Next, read the derivation the dictionary gives
for the word "flue." Now go back to "chimney."
The definition, "a flue for the smoke or gases
from a fire," now makes sense, so you use it in
sentences until you have a concept of it.*

chimney 1. ~~~
gases from a fire. 2. A glass
tube around the flame of a lamp.
3. A vent as in a cliff or volcano
~~~minata, fireplace

■ *You then clear the other definitions. If the
dictionary you are using has specialized or
obsolete definitions, you would skip them as
they aren't in common usage.*

around ~~~
3. A vent as in a cliff or volca~~~
[OFr. LL *caminata,* fireplace L.
caminus Gr. *kaminos,* furnace]
~~~**ey corner** corner or side of a

■ *Now clear up the derivation of the word.
You find that "chimney" originally came from
the Greek word "kaminos," which means
"furnace." If the word had any notes about its
use, synonyms or idioms, they would all be
cleared too. That would be the end of clearing
"chimney."*

*The above is the way any word should be
cleared. When words are understood,
communication can take place, and with
communication any given subject can be
understood.*

4. The next thing to do is to clear the derivation, which is the explanation of where the word came from originally. This will help you gain a basic understanding of the word.

5. Most dictionaries give the idioms of a word. An idiom is a phrase or expression whose meaning cannot be understood from the ordinary meanings of the words. For example, "give in" is an English idiom meaning "yield." Quite a few words in English have idiomatic uses and these are usually given in a dictionary after the definitions of the word itself. If there are idioms for the word that you are clearing, they are cleared as well.

6. Clear any other information given about the word, such as notes on its usage, synonyms, etc., so as to have a full understanding of the word. (A synonym is a word which has a similar but not the same meaning to another word, for example, "thin" and "lean.")

7. If you encounter a misunderstood word or symbol in the definition of a word being cleared, you must clear it right away using this same procedure and then return to the definition you were clearing. (Dictionary symbols and abbreviations are usually given in the front of the dictionary.) However, if you find yourself spending a lot of time clearing words within definitions of words, you should get a simpler dictionary. A good dictionary will enable you to clear a word without having to look up a lot of other ones in the process.

Simple Words

You might suppose at once that it is the *big* words or the technical words which are most misunderstood.

This is *not* the case.

Words like *a, the, exist, such* and other words that "everybody knows" are found with great frequency as misunderstood words when doing Word Clearing.

It takes a *big* dictionary to define these simple words fully. This is another oddity. The small dictionaries also suppose "everybody knows what that word means."

It is almost incredible to see that a university graduate has gone through years and years of study of complex subjects and yet does not know what "or" or "by" or "an" means. It has to be seen to be believed. Yet when cleaned up, his whole education turns from a solid mass of question marks to a clean useful view.

A test of schoolchildren in Johannesburg, South Africa, once showed that intelligence *decreased* with each new year of school!

The answer to the puzzle was simply that each year they added a few dozen more crushing misunderstood words onto an already confused vocabulary that no one ever got them to look up.

Stupidity *is* the effect of misunderstood words.

In those areas which give man the most trouble, you will find the most alteration of fact, the most confused and conflicting ideas and of course the greatest number of misunderstood words.

THE EARLIEST MISUNDERSTOOD WORD IN A SUBJECT IS A KEY TO LATER MISUNDERSTOOD WORDS IN THAT SUBJECT.

In studying a foreign language it is often found that the grammar words of one's *own* language that tell about the grammar in the foreign language are basic to not being able to learn the foreign language.

It is important that these words be cleared.

Methods of Word Clearing

Nine different methods for clearing the meanings of words have been developed in Scientology.

They cover various ways to locate the misunderstood words underlying a person's difficulties. These range from finding misunderstood words in the text one is studying, to clearing the key words relating to one's job, to even tracing down the words that were misunderstood in subjects studied years earlier!

Three of these Word Clearing methods that are very applicable in everyday life are given here.

Basic Word Clearing

Basic Word Clearing is the method of finding a misunderstood word by looking earlier in the text for a misunderstood word than where one is having trouble. This is the most basic method of Word Clearing used in Scientology.

A student must know how to keep himself tearing along successfully in his studies. He should be able to handle anything that slows or interferes with his progress. He applies the Study Technology to assist himself.

A student who uses Study Technology will look up each word he comes to that he doesn't understand and will never leave a word behind him that he doesn't know the meaning of.

If he runs into trouble, the student himself, his study partner or his instructor (in Scientology called a Supervisor) uses Basic Word Clearing to handle anything that slowed or interfered with his progress.

Waiting to become groggy or to "dope off" (feel tired, sleepy or foggy as though doped or drugged) as the only detection of misunderstood words before handling is waiting too long. If you have ever seen a student falling asleep over his book, then you have seen dope-off. Long before that point, someone should have made the student look for a misunderstood word. The time to look for the misunderstood word is as soon as the student slows down or isn't quite as "bright" as he was fifteen minutes before. It is not a misunderstood phrase or idea or concept but a misunderstood WORD. This always occurs before the subject itself is not understood.

Basic Word Clearing is done as follows:

1. The student is not flying along and is not so "bright" as he was or he may exhibit just plain lack of enthusiasm or be taking too long on the course or be yawning or disinterested or doodling or daydreaming, etc.

2. The student must then look earlier in the text for a misunderstood word. There is one always; there are no exceptions. It may be that the misunderstood word is two pages or more back, but it is always earlier in the text than where the student is now.

3. The word is found. The student recognizes it in looking back for it. Or, if the student can't find it, one can take words from the text that could be the misunderstood word and ask, "What does _____ mean?" to see if the student gives the correct definition.

4. The student looks up the word found in a dictionary and clears it per the steps of clearing a misunderstood word described above. He uses it verbally several times in sentences of his own composition until he has obviously demonstrated he understands the word by the composition of his sentences.

5. The student now reads the text that contained the misunderstood word. If he is not now "bright," eager to get on with it, feeling happier, etc., then there is another misunderstood word earlier in the text. This is found by repeating steps 2–5.

6. When the student is bright and feeling happier, he comes forward, studying the text from where the misunderstood word was to the area of the subject he did not understand (where step 1 began).

The student will now be enthusiastic about his study of the subject, and that is the end result of Basic Word Clearing. (The result won't be achieved if a misunderstood word was missed or if there is an earlier misunderstood word in the text. If so, repeat steps 2–5.) If the student is now enthusiastic, have him continue studying.

Good Word Clearing is a system of backtracking. You have to look earlier than the point where the student became dull or confused and you'll find that there's a word that he doesn't understand somewhere before the trouble started. If he doesn't brighten up when the word is found and cleared, there will be a misunderstood word even before that one.

This will be very clear to you if you understand that *if it is not resolving, the thing the student is apparently having trouble with is not the thing the student is having trouble with.* Otherwise, it would resolve, wouldn't it? If he knew what he didn't understand, he could resolve it himself. So to talk to him about what he thinks he doesn't understand just gets nowhere. The trouble is *earlier*.

In Basic Word Clearing, the student must look earlier in the text for a misunderstood word. It is always earlier in the text than where the student is now.

Zeroing In on the Word

The formula is to find out where the student wasn't having any trouble and find out where the student is now having trouble and the misunderstood word will be in between. It will be at the tag end—the last part—of where he wasn't having trouble.

Basic Word Clearing is tremendously effective when done as described here.

Reading Aloud Word Clearing

A highly effective method of finding the words a person doesn't understand in a book or other written material is called Reading Aloud Word Clearing.

A student, when reading by himself, often does not know he has gone past misunderstood words. But whenever he does go by misunderstood words, he will have trouble with what he is reading.

In Reading Aloud Word Clearing, one has the person read the material aloud. The person he reads to helps him find and clear any misunderstood words and is called, appropriately, a *word clearer*.

Reading Aloud Word Clearing is commonly done by two persons on a turnabout basis: one student is the word clearer and word clears the other student, and then they switch around and the student who was just word cleared becomes the word clearer and word clears his partner.

A word can be misunderstood in many different ways. It is important that these different types of misunderstood words are known to the person doing Reading Aloud Word Clearing. A word can be misunderstood because of:

1. A *false* (totally wrong) definition—The person reads or hears the word "cat" and thinks "cat" means "box." You can't get more wrong.

2. An *invented* definition—When young, the person was always called "a girl" by his pals when he refused to do anything daring. He invents the definition of "girl" to be "a cowardly person."

3. An *incorrect* definition—A person reads or hears the word "computer" and thinks it is a "typewriter." This is an incorrect meaning for "computer" even though a typewriter and a computer are both types of machines.

4. An *incomplete* definition—The person reads the word "office" and thinks it means "room." The definition of the word "office" is "the building, room or series of rooms in which the affairs of a business, professional person, branch of government, etc., are carried on." The person's definition of "office" is incomplete.

5. An *unsuitable* definition—The person sees a dash (–) in the sentence "I finished numbers 3–7 today." He thinks a dash is a minus sign, realizes you cannot subtract 7 from 3 and so cannot understand it.

Drafting?

DRAFTING IS IMPORTANT TO AN ARCHITECT

A misunderstood word can prevent the person's understanding of something.

As a result, he can appear to have no aptitude for doing certain things, much to his frustration and unhappiness.

Drafting!

DICTIONARY

But, locating and fully clearing misunderstood words on a subject restores the ability to <u>do</u> in the area.

Clearing up misunderstood words is the key to resolve any difficulties in any subject the person is studying.

6. A *homonymic* (one sound or symbol which has two or more distinctly separate meanings) definition—The person hears the word "period" in the sentence "It was a disorderly period in history" and knowing that "period" comes at the end of a sentence and means stop, supposes that the world ended at that point.

7. A *substitute* (synonym) definition—The person reads the word "portly" and thinks the definition of the word is "fat." "Fat" is a synonym for the word "portly." The person has a misunderstood because the word "portly" means "large and heavy in a dignified and stately way."

8. An *omitted* (missing) definition—The person hears the line "The food here is too rich." This person knows two definitions for the word "rich." He knows that "rich" means "having much money, land, goods, etc." and "wealthy people." Neither of these definitions make much sense to him in the sentence he has just heard. He cannot understand how food could have anything to do with having a lot of money. He does not know that "rich" in this sense means, "containing plenty of butter, eggs, flavoring, etc."

9. A *no*-definition—A no-definition is a "not-understood" word or symbol. The person reads the sentence "The business produced no lucre." No understanding occurs, as he has no definition for "lucre." The word means "riches; money: chiefly a scornful word, as in *filthy lucre.*"

10. A *rejected* definition—The person refuses to look up the definition of asterisk (*). On discussion, it turns out that every time he sees an asterisk on the page he knows the material will be "very hard to read" and is "literary," "difficult" and "very intellectual."

If a person has habitually gone past many, many misunderstood words in his reading or his education (which most everybody in this present culture has), not only will his ability to read be lowered but also his intelligence. What he himself writes and says won't be understood, what he reads and hears he won't understand, and he will be out of communication. The probability is that the world will look like a very peculiar place to him, he will feel that he is "not understood" (How true!) and life will look a bit miserable to him. He can even appear to others to be criminal. At best he will become a sort of robot or zombie. So you see, it is very important to clear misunderstood words.

Why Reading Aloud Word Clearing Works

A student who understands all the words on the page he is reading will be able to read the page aloud perfectly. He will feel bright and alert and will fully understand what he reads. But when a student passes a word or symbol he doesn't understand, the misunderstood causes an interruption of his voice or physical beingness (his physical state). His voice may change, or he may stumble on a word or make a face or squint his eyes or react in some other way.

This is easy to understand if you remember that a person can go blank after he passes a word or symbol he doesn't understand. He may make a mistake in his reading right there at the point of the misunderstood, or he may

Reading Aloud Word Clearing is a thorough method of locating misunderstood words.

These become apparent through stumbles, alterations or in other ways as the student reads.

continue reading past the misunderstood and make a mistake on a later word or symbol. He will feel duller and he will try to make up for the dull feeling by reading with more effort. This will always be expressed by a nonoptimum action of some kind which must be noted and handled at once by the word clearer.

A *nonoptimum* reaction is anything the student does besides read the page easily, naturally and perfectly. Examples of *some* of the nonoptimum reactions that may show up are:

1. Student adding a word or leaving out a word or changing a word in the sentence he is reading.

2. Student stumbling on a word or saying it incorrectly.

3. Student pausing or reading more slowly.

4. Student frowning or looking uncertain.

5. Student going stiff or tensing a body part, such as squinting his eyes or tightening the grip of his hands, or biting his lip or some other physical reaction.

6. Student reading with effort.

7. Student reading with a glib, robotic attitude (which is how he gets after he has been forced to read "correctly" by someone who doesn't know anything about misunderstood words).

Other manifestations can occur.

The above is not a complete list of reactions but is intended to give an idea of what to look for. In all fairness, one can stumble when reading if he is trying to read in a dim light or he is having eye trouble or the print or handwriting or penciled corrections in the text are very hard to make out. Thus, it is necessary to do Reading Aloud Word Clearing only in bright light, and if the fellow is supposed to be wearing glasses, he should be wearing glasses, and the material being word cleared must not contain smudges and deletions itself. All possible reasons why he cannot *see* the text and unclear text must be removed. Otherwise, the student will simply say he couldn't see it or the light was bad or some other wrong Why (reason or cause).

Any time the person makes an error in his reading or reacts in some nonoptimum way, a misunderstood word will *always* be found *before* that point or sometimes *at* that point itself.

Example: The student is reading the page aloud. He reads, "Raymond walked home slowly and thoughtfully," then he frowns. The word clearer signals a halt by saying, "That's it," and then asks, "Is there some word or symbol there that you didn't understand?" (*If* the student wonders why he was stopped, the word clearer tells him what reaction he noticed.)

The student looks over what he has read. He feels uncertain about the word "slowly." He tells this to the word clearer and the word "slowly" is looked up in the dictionary and used in sentences until the student fully understands it.

When the word that was misunderstood is located and cleared, the student will brighten up and will begin reading clearly and correctly once again.

How to Do It

1. *Student and Word Clearer Sit Across from Each Other.*

The student and the word clearer sit across from each other at a table or desk. Each person has his own copy of the text to be word cleared. The word clearer must be able to see the student *and* the page in front of him at the same time.

2. *Dictionaries Are Available.*

A good, simple dictionary and any other dictionaries the student may need are available. (Above all things, do not use what is called a "dinky dictionary." This is different than a simple well-expressed dictionary. A dinky dictionary is what you commonly get off the paperback racks in drugstores. It quite often defines word A as word B and then defines word B as word A. It also omits all the alternative definitions and all the technical definitions.)

3. *Student Recognition of Misunderstood Words.*

Before the student starts reading, he should be told that if he reads anything he doesn't fully understand he should tell the word clearer, or if he sees a word he doesn't know the meaning of, he should stop and look the word up and clear it instead of going on past it. The student should be encouraged to find and clear misunderstood words himself. The word clearer on this method would never prevent the student from clearing a word that the student recognizes as misunderstood. Reading Aloud Word Clearing brings about the ability to do this, so that the student will find and clear his own misunderstood words in the future.

4. *Student Reads the Text Aloud to the Word Clearer.*

The student reads the text aloud to the word clearer. While the student reads, the word clearer follows his own copy of the same text, watches the student and listens to him.

The word clearer must be very alert and see or hear any nonoptimum reactions of the student while he is reading.

5. *Nonoptimum Reaction Equals Misunderstood Word.*

A nonoptimum reaction by the student to what he is reading is the clue to the word clearer that the student has encountered a misunderstood word. The word clearer and student must now locate the exact misunderstood word or symbol. It will be found *before* or sometimes *at* the point the nonoptimum reaction occurred.

6. *Find the Misunderstood.*

If it is not obvious to the student that he has reacted and he just continues reading, the word clearer says, "That's it. Is there some word or symbol there that you didn't understand?" It is the duty of the word clearer to steer the student to the misunderstood. It is either at the point of the nonoptimum reaction or before it. The point is that the student must be steered onto it. And it then is looked up.

The student may be able to spot his misunderstood word right away and tell the word clearer what it is. Or he may have difficulty finding it and the word clearer will have to help him find it.

The word clearer helps the student by getting him to look earlier and earlier in the text from the point where he reacted until the misunderstood word is found. The word clearer can also spot-check the student. Spot-checking means choosing words from the text the student has already read and checking with him to see if he knows the definitions of those words. The word clearer would choose an earlier word and simply ask, "What is the definition of _____?"

If the student is uncertain about any word or gives a wrong definition, then that word is taken up and cleared in the dictionary.

7. *Clear the Word.*

Once the misunderstood is found it must be fully cleared in the dictionary. Use the procedure in "Steps to Clear a Word" covered on page 18.

8. *Read the Sentence Again.*

The word clearer then asks the student to read once again the sentence in the text in which the misunderstood word or symbol was found. The student does so, and if he reads it correctly with understanding, he continues reading the text. Any further nonoptimum reactions are handled by finding the next misunderstood word and clearing it, as above.

9. *Reading Aloud Is Continued Until the Text Has Been Completed.*

Reading Aloud Word Clearing is continued until the text to be word cleared is completed.

At this point, where two students are doing Reading Aloud Word Clearing on each other, they switch around and the student who just completed being word cleared becomes the word clearer.

The student goes through the same section of text and then goes on to the next fresh passage.

They take it in turns like this, word clearing it section by section until they have both finished the whole text.

Cautions and Tips

It occasionally happens that the students doing the Word Clearing get into a quarrel or upset. If this happens, you know that one of two things has happened. Either:

1. "Misunderstood words" that were really understood were forced off on the student, or

2. Actual misunderstood words were not detected and were passed by.

You can clean up any falsely looked-up words by asking the student if he was made to look up words he understood. If this is the case, he will brighten up and tell you the word or words he was wrongly made to clear. This done, the Word Clearing can be resumed.

If the above doesn't handle it, then one knows that misunderstood words have been missed. Have the word clearer take the student back to when he was last doing well and then come forward in the text, following Reading Aloud Word Clearing procedure, picking up the missed misunderstood words. It will usually be found that several misunderstood words have been missed, not just one.

The end result of well-done Reading Aloud Word Clearing is a student who is certain he has no misunderstood words on that material so that he can easily study the material and apply it.

Reading Aloud Word Clearing is a great civilization saver.

It is vital that Reading Aloud Word Clearing is done correctly, exactly by the book. Otherwise, people will be denied the enormous wins that can be attained with it.

Special Reading Aloud Word Clearing

Whenever one is working with children or foreign-language persons or people who are semiliterate, Special Reading Aloud Word Clearing is used.

As in the Reading Aloud method, the person is made to read *aloud* to find out what he is doing.

It is a very simple method.

Another copy of the same text must also be followed by the word clearer as the person reads.

Startling things can be observed.

The person may omit the word "is" whenever it occurs. The person doesn't read it. He may have some strange meaning for it like "Israel" (actual occurrence).

He may omit "didn't" each time it occurs and the reason may trace to not knowing what the apostrophe is (actual occurrence).

He may call one word quite another word such as "stop" for "happen" or "green" for "mean."

He may hesitate over certain words.

In Special Reading Aloud Word Clearing, the person reads aloud and each time he hesitates, has a physical reaction or alters a word, the word clearer helps him find and define the misunderstood word.

The procedure is:

1. Have him read aloud.

2. Note each omission or word change or hesitation or frown as he reads and take it up at once.

3. Correct it by looking it up for him or explaining it to him.

4. Have him go on reading, noting the next omission, word change or hesitation or frown.

5. Repeat steps 2–4.

By doing this a person can be brought up to literacy.

His next actions would be learning how to use a dictionary and look up words.

Then a simple grammar text.

A very backward student can be boosted up to literacy by this Word Clearing method.

Applying the Technology of Study

Study Technology is a bridge to an education that will serve a student long after he leaves the classroom.

The difference between the "bright" student and the "dull" one, the student who is very, very fast and the one who is very, very slow, is really only the difference between the *careful* student and the *careless* student.

The careful student applies the technology of study. He studies with an intention to learn something. He handles any of the barriers to study which appear as he is working with his materials. If he is reading down a paragraph and suddenly realizes that he doesn't have a clue what he is reading about, he goes back and finds out where he got tangled up. Just before that there is a word he didn't understand. If he is a careful student, he doesn't continue—not until he finds out what that word is and what it means.

That is a careful student, and his brightness on the subject is dependent upon the degree he applies this technology. It isn't dependent on any native talent or anything else. It is his command of the subject of study that makes the difference.

This booklet is far from all there is to Study Technology. It is a comprehensive subject. But with what you have read in these pages, you now have the tools to study anything more successfully and help others do the same.■

PRACTICAL EXERCISES

Here are exercises you can do to increase your ability to apply Study Technology. These will help you become proficient in your own studies and in helping others with anything they are trying to learn.

1 Think of someone you have seen or known who felt he already knew all about some subject. How would this attitude affect the person's ability to actually learn something new about that subject?

2 How would you handle these situations?

a. A friend is learning about different types of trees but has no idea what they look like. There are no actual trees nearby that can be shown to him. How could you help him?

b. In learning how to swim, a friend just learned to float in the water and is now being taught to swim across the pool, but is having a great deal of trouble with this. What could you do to help him?

c. A friend has been taking a course on how to manage his money, but has now decided he does not want to continue or go back to class. What should you do to handle this?

3 Think of or find a word you know you do not understand or are unsure of and clear it, using a dictionary.

4 Go back through the section "Barriers to Study," looking for and clearing any words you do not fully understand and restudying the section as you go.

5 Do Basic Word Clearing on yourself.

6 Do Basic Word Clearing on another person.

7 Drill Reading Aloud Word Clearing. Find another student or a friend to do this drill with you. One of you will be Student A and the other will be Student B. Decide who is going to be Student A and who is going to be Student B.

a. Student A (as word clearer) word clears Student B on the following paragraph, using Reading Aloud. Use a simple dictionary.

The quick brown fox jumped over the lazy dog. The dog was supposed to be guarding the chickens but had gone to sleep. The fox sneaked into the chicken coop without anyone noticing.

b. Student B (as word clearer) word clears Student A on the following paragraphs, using Reading Aloud. Use a simple dictionary.

The quick brown fox jumped over the lazy dog. The dog was supposed to be guarding the chickens but had gone to sleep. The fox sneaked into the chicken coop without anyone noticing.

As soon as the chickens noticed him they all made a dreadful row. The fox had to move very quickly; he grabbed hold of the nearest chicken by her neck and slunk off out of the coop.

c. Student A (as word clearer) word clears Student B on the following paragraphs, using Reading Aloud. Use a simple dictionary.

As soon as the chickens noticed him they all made a dreadful row. The fox had to move very quickly; he grabbed hold of the nearest chicken by her neck and slunk off out of the coop.

The farmer's wife came running out of the house when she heard the din, wondering what could possibly be going on with her chickens. She saw the fox disappearing into the nearby woods with the chicken.

d. Student B (as word clearer) word clears Student A on the following paragraphs, using Reading Aloud. Use a simple dictionary.

The farmer's wife came running out of the house when she heard the din, wondering what could possibly be going on with her chickens. She saw the fox disappearing into the nearby woods with the chicken.

She shrieked loudly and looked around for the dog whose prime duty it was to prevent this sort of occurrence. The dog looked quite abashed. The farmer's wife spent the next few minutes violently upbraiding him for his apathetic behavior.

e. Student A (as word clearer) word clears Student B on the following paragraph, using Reading Aloud. Use a simple dictionary.

She shrieked loudly and looked around for the dog whose prime duty it was to prevent this sort of occurrence. The dog looked quite abashed. The farmer's wife spent the next few minutes violently upbraiding him for his apathetic behavior.

8 Find someone who could benefit from Reading Aloud Word Clearing and do this to a satisfactory end result.

RESULTS FROM APPLICATION

Study Technology, widely used from American universities to South African township schools, routinely demonstrates its workability in program after program.

In rural Alabama, children ranging in age from eight to sixteen took part in a seven-week program utilizing Study Technology for the stated purpose of increasing reading vocabulary and comprehension. Pre- and post-program standardized tests revealed an average increase of eight months per student in vocabulary and comprehension. One fourteen-year-old boy improved from a second grade level to sixth grade level in five and a half weeks on the program. This level of increase is virtually unheard of.

In London, a group of pupils received a short course in Study Technology consisting of approximately nine hours of instruction over a twelve-day period, while a control group received no instruction in Study Technology. Both groups otherwise continued their routine studies and both were tested before and after. The experimental group became an astonishing average of 1.29 years higher in reading ability after twelve days of instruction. The control group showed virtually no difference (0.03 decrease) in the second test. These impressive results speak for themselves.

The benefits of the Education Alive program in southern Africa have been

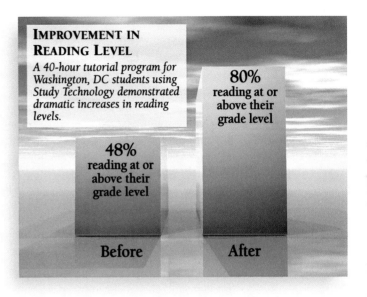

IMPROVEMENT IN READING LEVEL
A 40-hour tutorial program for Washington, DC students using Study Technology demonstrated dramatic increases in reading levels.

48% reading at or above their grade level

80% reading at or above their grade level

Before   After

validated by several studies in Bulawayo, Zimbabwe and the Transvaal, South Africa. One study demonstrated a 1.2 year improvement in reading ability over the course of a three-week program. Another program delivered over a four-week period yielded improvements averaging 1.8 years in reading ability. Another three-week program in the Transkei homeland in South Africa, showed a 2.3 year average improvement. A program run in an underprivileged high school resulted in a 91 percent pass rate on the country's Department of Education high-school examinations, compared to 27 percent in a control group. In South Africa, where 50 percent of the population is illiterate, this program brings about vitally needed improvement.

Compare these positive results to what is occurring elsewhere in school systems throughout the world: some inner city US high schools have drop-out rates approaching 50 percent; 42 percent of those surveyed in Great Britain could not add up the price of a hamburger, French fries, apple pie and coffee; and 700,000 students graduated from US high schools last year who were not literate enough to read their diplomas. Behind these figures lie many stories of personal frustration, broken dreams, low-quality workmanship, rising crime and bleak futures.

The stories of the people which follow are different. Luckily, these people from around the world found out about Study Technology and applied it and changed their lives and the lives of others for the better.

In Springfield, Virginia, a couple were distressed about their son's failures in school and problems at home. After being introduced to Study Technology and enrolling their son in a school which uses it, they wrote the following letter:

"Before Richard started at your school, and as a result of his inability to respond to the teaching methods of the Washington, DC public schools, he was a frustrated, unadjusted kid. Through the guidance and counseling provided, we were able to learn how to assist Richard in becoming a better person. More importantly, you sparked a renewed interest in him. He obtained the basic educational skills he had missed during the two years he spent in public

schools. For the first time in two years, Richard wanted to go to school every day! He took the initiative to read books on his own. He became interested in various academic subjects, including science and geography. From the time his two cousins graduated from a prestigious high school, it had been Richard's dream to attend the same school. After learning Study Technology, he was accepted for enrollment in this school. We thank you from the bottom of our hearts for the big part you played in helping Richard to reach his goal."

Beside herself with worry, a London mother sought help for her ten-year-old son who was having great difficulty in school and could not concentrate. His teachers wanted to give him drugs. Instead, his mother found a tutorial program utilizing Study Technology. After the boy spent a short while on the program, his tutor wrote:

"During his first Saturday on the program, the boy spent three hours learning the basics of Study Technology. The boy's mother rang me during the next week as she noticed an immediate improvement and could not believe the change that had come over her son—the boy was doing his homework with no difficulties. The next Saturday, the boy returned to the program and learned more about how to study. A few days later the boy's mother told me that she received a call from his teachers wondering what had occurred with him. They had noticed such a change, they wanted to know what was going on. The youngster's problems would not have been solved by

drugs. It was simply that no one had ever taught him how to study."

A couple in Oregon were distraught about their eleven-year-old daughter who was barely reading at a second grade level and who had very low self-esteem. After her daughter started attending a school which uses Study Technology, the girl's mother wrote:

"My heart wrenched when my daughter came out of the room used for the entrance exam which she took on arriving at summer school. Tears streamed down her face and she asked for her green-tinted lenses which she thought she needed in order to read. She had scored very poorly, but in spite of reservations from all concerned she was given a chance to begin the summer program.

"At that moment the cumulative graph of her life which had been plummeting steeply took a sharp turn upward and it has been climbing ever since. She has now been at summer school for some months and the changes we have seen in her are nothing short of miraculous.

"She is reading now on her own, and even finds it hard to put her books down. She is back on track and has become a confident, happy kid, a great kid who will no doubt make an enormous contribution to the world—a contribution she could never

have made if it were not for the study method of Mr. Hubbard and this incredible school you are creating! Thanks to every one of you for your efforts, your commitment and your vision."

A seven-year-old boy was having a hard time on his studies. He was studying and restudying the same materials for about six months. Fortunately, his mother knew Study Technology and realized that his teacher was not finding and correcting the real barriers and problems her son was running into.

"I have a very busy schedule with my own job and duties but I got him to bring home the materials he had been studying and I found what the real problem was. That was two months ago. The result is that he has become a model student in his class now. He no longer goofs off or gives others a hard time. He loves his studies and has been completing his assignments in record time. He came to me two nights ago and was spelling words which he had studied and properly cleared the definitions of. I know I could not even read when I was his age, let alone spell words like Antarctica, nurseries, patterns, penguin, polar bear, iceberg, etc. I realized that I had possibly salvaged his whole study future with what I had done earlier to resolve his study problems."

GLOSSARY

clay demonstration: a model made out of clay by a student to demonstrate an action, definition, object or principle. Also called a "clay demo."

confront: to face without flinching or avoiding. The ability to confront is actually the ability to be there comfortably and perceive.

demonstration kit: a kit composed of various small objects such as corks, caps, paper clips, pen tops, rubber bands, etc. A student uses these small objects to represent the various parts of something he is studying about. The objects can be moved about to show the mechanics and actions of a given concept and help the student understand it. Also called a "demo kit."

doingness: the performance of some action or activity.

dope off: feel tired, sleepy or foggy as though doped or drugged.

gradient: a gradual approach to something taken step by step, level by level, each step or level being, of itself, easily attainable—so that finally, complicated and difficult activities can be achieved with relative ease. The term *gradient* also applies to each of the steps taken in such an approach.

individuate: separate oneself from someone, a group, etc., and withdraw from involvement with it.

mass: the actual physical objects, the things of life; as opposed to significance. *See also* **significance** in this glossary.

misunderstood word: a word which is *not* understood or *wrongly* understood.

Scientology: an applied religious philosophy developed by L. Ron Hubbard. It is the study and handling of the spirit in relationship to itself, universes and other life. The word *Scientology* comes from the Latin *scio,* which means "know" and the Greek word *logos,* meaning "the word or outward form by which the inward thought is expressed and made known." Thus, Scientology means knowing about knowing.

significance: the meaning or ideas or theory of something, as opposed to its mass.

win: the accomplishment of any desired improvement. Examples of wins would be a person increasing his ability to communicate, experiencing an increased feeling of well-being or gaining more certainty about some area of his life.

word clear: define, using a dictionary, any words not fully understood in the material a person is studying.

word clearer: a person who helps another person find and clear any misunderstood words.

Word Clearing: that body of Scientology procedures used to locate words a person has misunderstood in subjects he has studied and get the words defined by looking them up in a dictionary.

ABOUT L. RON HUBBARD

Born in Tilden, Nebraska on March 13, 1911, his road of discovery and dedication to his fellows began at an early age. By the age of nineteen, he had traveled more than a quarter of a million miles, examining the cultures of Java, Japan, India and the Philippines.

Returning to the United States in 1929, Ron resumed his formal education and studied mathematics, engineering and the then new field of nuclear physics—all providing vital tools for continued research. To finance that research, Ron embarked upon a literary career in the early 1930s, and soon became one of the most widely read authors of popular fiction. Yet never losing sight of his primary goal, he continued his mainline research through extensive travel and expeditions.

With the advent of World War II, he entered the United States Navy as a lieutenant (junior grade) and served as commander of antisubmarine corvettes. Left partially blind and lame from injuries sustained during combat, he was diagnosed as permanently disabled by 1945. Through application of his theories on the mind, however, he was not only able to help fellow servicemen, but also to regain his own health.

After five more years of intensive research, Ron's discoveries were presented to the world in *Dianetics: The Modern Science of Mental Health*. The first popular handbook on the human mind expressly written for the man in the street, *Dianetics* ushered in a new era of hope for mankind and a new phase of life for its author. He did, however, not cease his research, and as breakthrough after breakthrough was carefully codified through late 1951, the applied religious philosophy of Scientology was born.

Because Scientology explains the whole of life, there is no aspect of man's existence that L. Ron Hubbard's subsequent work did not address. Residing variously in the United States and England, his continued research brought forth solutions to such social ills as declining educational standards and pandemic drug abuse.

All told, L. Ron Hubbard's works on Scientology and Dianetics total forty million words of recorded lectures, books and writings. Together, these constitute the legacy of a lifetime that ended on January 24, 1986. Yet the passing of L. Ron Hubbard in no way constituted an end; for with a hundred million of his books in circulation and millions of people daily applying his technologies for betterment, it can truly be said the world still has no greater friend.■

CHURCHES OF SCIENTOLOGY

Contact Your Nearest Church or Organization or visit www.volunteerministers.org

UNITED STATES

ALBUQUERQUE

Church of Scientology
8106 Menaul Boulevard NE
Albuquerque, New Mexico
87110

ANN ARBOR

Church of Scientology
66 E. Michigan Avenue
Battle Creek, Michigan 49017

ATLANTA

Church of Scientology
1611 Mt. Vernon Road
Dunwoody, Georgia 30338

AUSTIN

Church of Scientology
2200 Guadalupe
Austin, Texas 78705

BOSTON

Church of Scientology
448 Beacon Street
Boston, Massachusetts 02115

BUFFALO

Church of Scientology
836 N. Main Street
Buffalo, New York 14202

CHICAGO

Church of Scientology
3011 North Lincoln Avenue
Chicago, Illinois 60657-4207

CINCINNATI

Church of Scientology
215 West 4th Street, 5th Floor
Cincinnati, Ohio 45202-2670

CLEARWATER

Church of Scientology
Flag Service Organization
210 South Fort Harrison Avenue
Clearwater, Florida 33756

Foundation Church of
Scientology
Flag Ship Service Organization
c/o *Freewinds* Relay Office
118 North Fort Harrison Avenue
Clearwater, Florida
33755-4013

COLUMBUS

Church of Scientology
30 North High Street
Columbus, Ohio 43215

DALLAS

Church of Scientology
Celebrity Centre Dallas
1850 North Buckner Boulevard
Dallas, Texas 75228

DENVER

Church of Scientology
3385 South Bannock Street
Englewood, Colorado 80110

DETROIT

Church of Scientology
28000 Middlebelt Road
Farmington Hills, Michigan
48334

HONOLULU

Church of Scientology
1146 Bethel Street
Honolulu, Hawaii 96813

KANSAS CITY

Church of Scientology
3619 Broadway
Kansas City, Missouri 64111

LAS VEGAS

Church of Scientology
846 East Sahara Avenue
Las Vegas, Nevada 89104

Church of Scientology
Celebrity Centre Las Vegas
4850 W. Flamingo Road, Suite 10
Las Vegas, Nevada 89103

LONG ISLAND

Church of Scientology
64 Bethpage Road
Hicksville, New York
11801-2850

LOS ANGELES AND VICINITY

Church of Scientology
of Los Angeles
4810 Sunset Boulevard
Los Angeles, California 90027

Church of Scientology
1451 Irvine Boulevard
Tustin, California 92680

Church of Scientology
1277 East Colorado Boulevard
Pasadena, California 91106

Church of Scientology
15643 Sherman Way
Van Nuys, California 91406

Church of Scientology
American Saint Hill
Organization
1413 L. Ron Hubbard Way
Los Angeles, California 90027

Church of Scientology
American Saint Hill
Foundation
1413 L. Ron Hubbard Way
Los Angeles, California 90027

Church of Scientology
Advanced Organization
of Los Angeles
1306 L. Ron Hubbard Way
Los Angeles, California 90027

Church of Scientology
Celebrity Centre International
5930 Franklin Avenue
Hollywood, California 90028

LOS GATOS

Church of Scientology
650 Saratoga Avenue
San Jose, California 95117

MIAMI

Church of Scientology
120 Giralda Avenue
Coral Gables, Florida 33134

MINNEAPOLIS

Church of Scientology
Twin Cities
1011 Nicollet Mall
Minneapolis, Minnesota 55403

MOUNTAIN VIEW

Church of Scientology
2483 Old Middlefield Way
Mountain View, California
94043

NASHVILLE

Church of Scientology
Celebrity Centre Nashville
1204 16th Avenue South
Nashville, Tennessee 37212

NEW HAVEN
Church of Scientology
909 Whalley Avenue
New Haven, Connecticut
06515-1728

NEW YORK CITY
Church of Scientology
227 West 46th Street
New York, New York
10036-1409

Church of Scientology
Celebrity Centre New York
65 East 82nd Street
New York, New York 10028

ORLANDO
Church of Scientology
1830 East Colonial Drive
Orlando, Florida 32803-4729

PHILADELPHIA
Church of Scientology
1315 Race Street
Philadelphia, Pennsylvania
19107

PHOENIX
Church of Scientology
2702 N. 44th St., Suite A100
Mesa, Arizona 85201

PORTLAND
Church of Scientology
2636 NE Sandy Boulevard
Portland, Oregon 97232-2342

Church of Scientology
Celebrity Centre Portland
708 SW Salmon Street
Portland, Oregon 97205

SACRAMENTO
Church of Scientology
825 15th Street
Sacramento, California
95814-2096

SALT LAKE CITY
Church of Scientology
1931 South 1100 East
Salt Lake City, Utah 84106

SAN DIEGO
Church of Scientology
1330 4th Avenue
San Diego, California 92101

SAN FRANCISCO
Church of Scientology
701 Montgomery Street
San Francisco, California
94111

SAN JOSE
Church of Scientology
80 East Rosemary Street
San Jose, California 95112

SANTA BARBARA
Church of Scientology
524 State Street
Santa Barbara, California
93101

SEATTLE
Church of Scientology
2226 3rd Avenue
Seattle, Washington 98121

ST. LOUIS
Church of Scientology
6901 Delmar Boulevard
University City, Missouri
63130

TAMPA
Church of Scientology
3102 N. Havana Avenue
Tampa, Florida 33607

WASHINGTON, DC
Founding Church of
   Scientology
of Washington, DC
1701 20th Street NW
Washington, DC 20009

PUERTO RICO
HATO REY
Dianetics Center of
   Puerto Rico
272 JT Piñero Avenue
Hyde Park
San Juan, Puerto Rico 00918

CANADA
EDMONTON
Church of Scientology
10206 106th Street NW
Edmonton, Alberta
Canada T5J 1H7

KITCHENER
Church of Scientology
104 King Street West
   2nd Floor
Kitchener, Ontario
Canada N2G 1A6

MONTREAL
Church of Scientology
4489 Papineau Street
Montreal, Quebec
Canada H2H 1T7

OTTAWA
Church of Scientology
150 Rideau Street, 2nd Floor
Ottawa, Ontario
Canada K1N 5X6

QUEBEC
Church of Scientology
350 Bd Chareste Est
Quebec, Quebec
Canada G1K 3H5

TORONTO
Church of Scientology
696 Yonge Street, 2nd Floor
Toronto, Ontario
Canada M4Y 2A7

VANCOUVER
Church of Scientology
401 West Hastings Street
Vancouver, British Columbia
Canada V6B 1L5

WINNIPEG
Church of Scientology
315 Garry Street, Suite 210
Winnipeg, Manitoba
Canada R3B 2G7

UNITED KINGDOM
BIRMINGHAM
Church of Scientology
8 Ethel Street
Winston Churchill House
Birmingham, England B2 4BG

BRIGHTON
Church of Scientology
Third Floor, 79-83 North Street
Brighton, Sussex
England BN1 1ZA

EAST GRINSTEAD
Church of Scientology
Saint Hill Foundation
Saint Hill Manor
East Grinstead, West Sussex
England RH19 4JY

Advanced Organization
   Saint Hill
Saint Hill Manor
East Grinstead, West Sussex
England RH19 4JY

EDINBURGH
Hubbard Academy of Personal
   Independence
20 Southbridge
Edinburgh, Scotland EH1 1LL

LONDON
Church of Scientology
68 Tottenham Court Road
London, England W1P 0BB

Church of Scientology
Celebrity Centre London
42 Leinster Gardens
London, England W2 3AN

MANCHESTER

Church of Scientology
258 Deansgate
Manchester, England M3 4BG

PLYMOUTH

Church of Scientology
41 Ebrington Street
Plymouth, Devon
England PL4 9AA

SUNDERLAND

Church of Scientology
51 Fawcett Street
Sunderland, Tyne and Wear
England SR1 1RS

AUSTRALIA

ADELAIDE

Church of Scientology
24–28 Waymouth Street
Adelaide, South Australia
Australia 5000

BRISBANE

Church of Scientology
106 Edward Street, 2nd Floor
Brisbane, Queensland
Australia 4000

CANBERRA

Church of Scientology
43–45 East Row
Canberra City, ACT
Australia 2601

MELBOURNE

Church of Scientology
42–44 Russell Street
Melbourne, Victoria
Australia 3000

PERTH

Church of Scientology
108 Murray Street, 1st Floor
Perth, Western Australia
Australia 6000

SYDNEY

Church of Scientology
201 Castlereagh Street
Sydney, New South Wales
Australia 2000

Church of Scientology
Advanced Organization
    Saint Hill Australia,
    New Zealand and Oceania
19–37 Greek Street
Glebe, New South Wales
Australia 2037

NEW ZEALAND

AUCKLAND

Church of Scientology
159 Queen Street, 3rd Floor
Auckland 1, New Zealand

AFRICA

BULAWAYO

Church of Scientology
Southampton House, Suite 202
Main Street and 9th Avenue
Bulawayo, Zimbabwe

CAPE TOWN

Church of Scientology
Ground Floor, Dorlane House
39 Roeland Street
Cape Town 8001, South Africa

DURBAN

Church of Scientology
20 Buckingham Terrace
Westville, Durban 3630
South Africa

HARARE

Church of Scientology
404-409 Pockets Building
50 Jason Moyo Avenue
Harare, Zimbabwe

JOHANNESBURG

Church of Scientology
4th Floor, Budget House
130 Main Street
Johannesburg 2001
South Africa

Church of Scientology
No. 108 1st Floor,
    Bordeaux Centre
Gordon Road, Corner Jan
    Smuts Avenue
Blairgowrie, Randburg 2125
South Africa

PORT ELIZABETH

Church of Scientology
2 St. Christopher's
27 Westbourne Road Central
Port Elizabeth 6001
South Africa

PRETORIA

Church of Scientology
307 Ancore Building
Corner Jeppe and Esselen Streets
Sunnyside, Pretoria 0002
South Africa

SCIENTOLOGY MISSIONS

INTERNATIONAL OFFICE

Scientology Missions
    International
6331 Hollywood Boulevard
Suite 501
Los Angeles, California
90028-6314

UNITED STATES

Scientology Missions
    International
Western United States Office
1308 L. Ron Hubbard Way
Los Angeles, California 90027

Scientology Missions
    International
Eastern United States Office
349 W. 48th Street
New York, New York 10036

Scientology Missions
    International
Flag Land Base Office
210 South Fort Harrison Avenue
Clearwater, Florida 33756

AFRICA

Scientology Missions
    International
African Office
6th Floor, Budget House
130 Main Street
Johannesburg 2001
South Africa

AUSTRALIA, NEW ZEALAND AND OCEANIA

Scientology Missions
    International
Australian, New Zealand
    and Oceanian Office
201 Castlereagh Street,
    3rd Floor
Sydney, New South Wales
Australia 2000

CANADA

Scientology Missions
    International
Canadian Office
696 Yonge Street
Toronto, Ontario
Canada M4Y 2A7

UNITED KINGDOM

Scientology Missions
    International
United Kingdom Office
Saint Hill Manor
East Grinstead, West Sussex
England RH19 4JY

To obtain any books or cassettes by L. Ron Hubbard which are not available at your local organization, contact any of the following publications organizations worldwide:

Bridge Publications, Inc.
4751 Fountain Avenue
Los Angeles, California 90029
www.bridgepub.com

Continental Publications Liaison Office
696 Yonge Street
Toronto, Ontario
Canada M4Y 2A7

NEW ERA Publications International ApS
Store Kongensgade 53
1264 Copenhagen K
Denmark
www.newerapublications.com

ERA DINÁMICA Editores, S.A. de C.V.
Tonalá #210
Delegación Cuauhtemoc
México, D.F., C.P. 06760

NEW ERA Publications UK Ltd.
Saint Hill Manor
East Grinstead, West Sussex
England RH19 4JY

NEW ERA Publications Australia Pty Ltd.
Level 1, 61–65 Wentworth
Avenue
Surry Hills, New South Wales
Australia 2010

Continental Publications Pty Ltd.
6th Floor, Budget House
130 Main Street
Johannesburg 2001
South Africa

NEW ERA Publications Italia S.r.l.
Via Cadorna, 61
20090 Vimodrone (MI), Italy

NEW ERA Publications Deutschland GmbH
Hittfelder Kirchweg 5A
21220 Seevetal-Maschen
Germany

NEW ERA Publications Rep. para Iberia
Apartado postal 909
28080 Madrid, Spain

NEW ERA Publications Japan, Inc.
Sakai SS bldg 2F, 4-38-15
Higashi-Ikebukuro
Toshima-ku, Tokyo, Japan
170-0013

NEW ERA Publications Group
St. Presnenskyval, 28, Building 1
123557 Moscow, Russia

NEW ERA Publications Central European Office
1438 Budapest
Pf. 351
Hungary

Bridge Publications, Inc.
4751 Fountain Avenue, Los Angeles, California 90029
ISBN 0-88404-908-6

An L. RON HUBBARD Publication